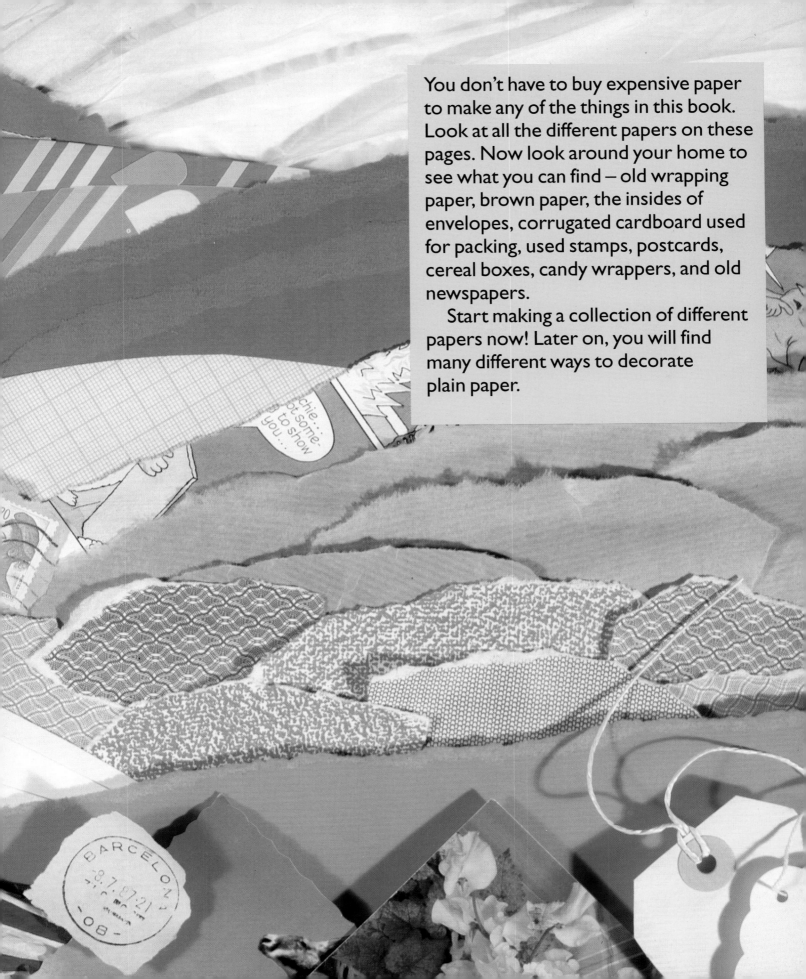

You don't have to buy expensive paper to make any of the things in this book. Look at all the different papers on these pages. Now look around your home to see what you can find — old wrapping paper, brown paper, the insides of envelopes, corrugated cardboard used for packing, used stamps, postcards, cereal boxes, candy wrappers, and old newspapers.

Start making a collection of different papers now! Later on, you will find many different ways to decorate plain paper.

EQUIPMENT

When you have gathered together a collection of different papers, you are almost ready to start! All of the things on these pages are used somewhere in this book for cutting, gluing, decorating, and assembling. You will probably be able to find most of them in your home, but you may have to buy some of them from craft or toy stores.

Be very careful when using scissors and craft knives – ask for help if you have any problems with cutting! Always use a piece of thick cardboard or linoleum when you are cutting with a sharp knife.

straws for spattering and decorating

ruler for straight lines

scissors

paint and brushes for decorating paper

toothpicks for flower stems

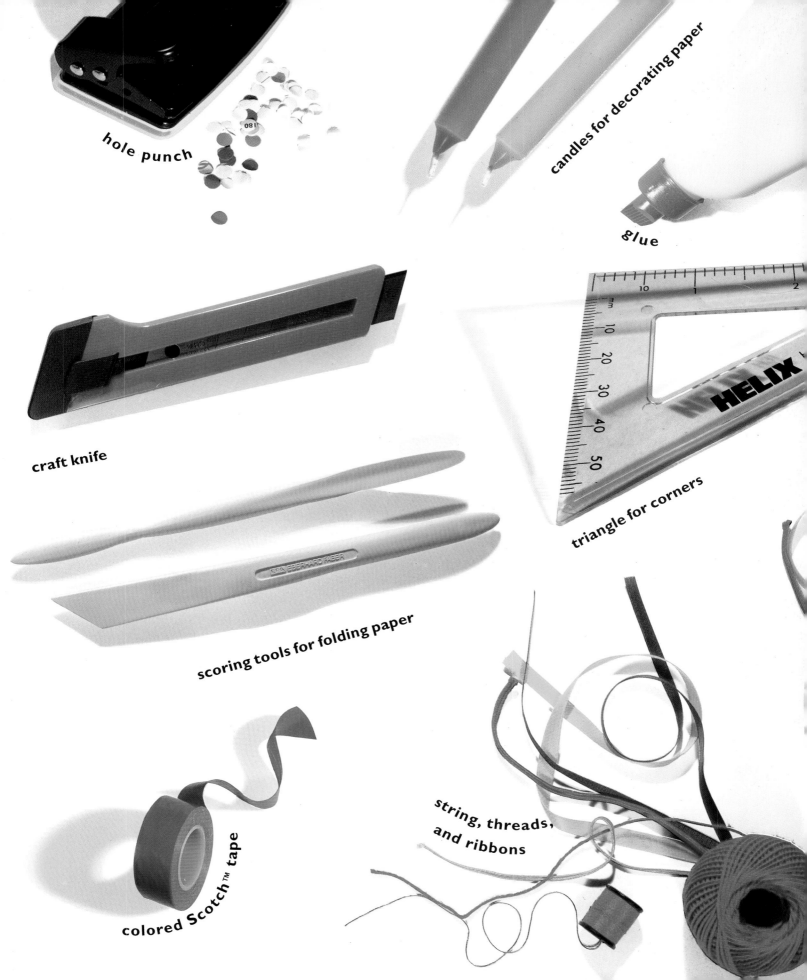

hole punch

candles for decorating paper

glue

craft knife

triangle for corners

scoring tools for folding paper

colored Scotch™ tape

string, threads, and ribbons

Paper Curls

Cut a long, thin strip of colored paper. Wrap the strip tightly around a pencil or knitting needle. Pull the pencil or needle out and you will have a paper curl.

Paper Beads

Glue two sheets of colored paper together. Tear out triangles and roll them up tightly, starting at the wide end.

Crumpled Paper

Give paper an interesting texture by crumpling it up. When you are collecting papers, look for paper that has already been crumpled up.

Weaving Paper

Cut out some long, thin strips of different colored paper. Weave the strips in and out, as in the picture. If you want the strips to stay in position, glue them onto a backing sheet.

Glue and Tear

You can make paper stronger by gluing two layers together. If you glue two different colors together and then tear out shapes, you will get an interesting edge. If you glue three or more layers of paper together, you will get an even stronger paper — more like thin cardboard.

Accordion Folds

Take a long, thin strip of paper and practice making accordion folds, or pleats. They can be as large or as small as you like. Later on, you will see how to use pleated paper to make jewelry and paper flowers.

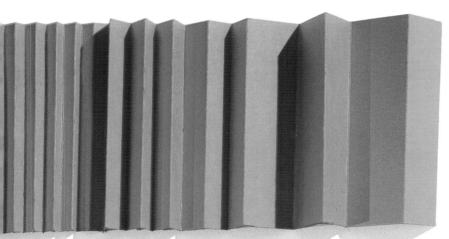

Cutting, Punching, and Tearing

Cutting paper gives a smooth edge, while tearing leaves a ragged edge. Both methods give interesting effects and are used in this book. Use a hole punch to punch small, round holes. Keep the pieces — they may be useful!

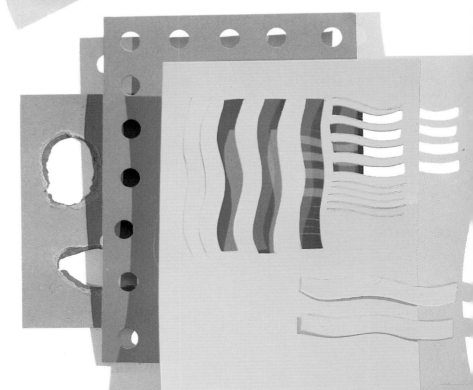

If you look carefully at this picture, you will see that it is made almost entirely from different kinds of paper.

The papers here include newspaper, insides of envelopes, brown paper, wrapping paper, wax paper, and tissue paper, as well as plastic straws, and aluminum foil. Look around your home to see how many different kinds of paper you can find.

Draw a rough sketch of your idea and decide which papers will be best.

Cut and tear the papers into shapes and glue them in position, starting with the background.

Remember that you can bend, curl, and crumple paper and thin cardboard to make interesting shapes. Look at pages 6 and 7 to find out how to weave paper and make accordion folds.

Make the paste from the recipe opposite and put some into small containers. Add some paint and mix well. Cover a sheet of paper with paste paint. Make cardboard scrapers like the ones at the bottom of the page and use them to make patterns in the paste paint. When the paste paint is dry, you can use the paper to make jewelry, cards, wrapping paper, and shopping bags.

Paste Recipe
1 cup flour
3 cups water

1. In a saucepan, mix a little of the water with the flour to make a smooth paste.
2. Add the rest of the water and ask a grown-up to heat the mixture until it boils – stirring all the time. When it is boiling, turn the heat down and let the mixture simmer until the paste thickens. Leave the mixture until it is cold.

Here are some examples of different methods for decorating paper. Turn over the page to see the results.

Sponge Printing
Try dipping differently shaped sponges – large and small – into fairly thick paint. Press the sponges onto the paper.

Object Printing
Look for objects that have an interesting shape or a raised texture. Dip them into fairly thick paint and press onto the paper.

Wax and Paint
Make a pattern on the paper with wax crayons or candles. Paint over the wax marks with medium-thick paint. The paint will not stay where the wax marks are.

Crumpled Paper
Crumple up a small piece of paper and dip it into thick paint. Press it onto the paper to make a print.

Spattering
This is a very quick and easy method for decorating paper. Dip a large paintbrush into thick paint and either flick or shake it over the paper.

DECORATING PAPER 2

Here are some papers that have been decorated using the methods described on page 12.

Experiment with the suggestions in this book and try out your own ideas too.

(1) (6) Spatter painting

(2) (9) Crumpled-paper printing

(3) Crumpled paper

(4) Sponge printing

(5) (8) Paste paper

(7) Wax and paint

(10) Sponge and object printing

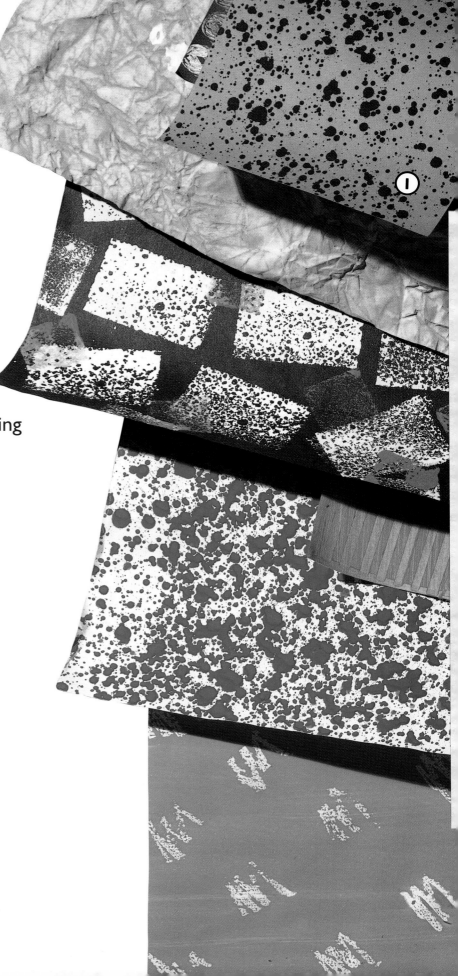

You don't need paints or colored pencils to make these cards and gift tags! All you need is colored paper, glue, scissors, and a craft knife. Ask a grown-up to help.

Slit and Slot Card

Fold a sheet of colored paper in half. Make slits from the top to the bottom, using a craft knife. Leave a border of at least I inch (2.5 cm) around the card. Weave different colored strips of paper in and out of the slits.

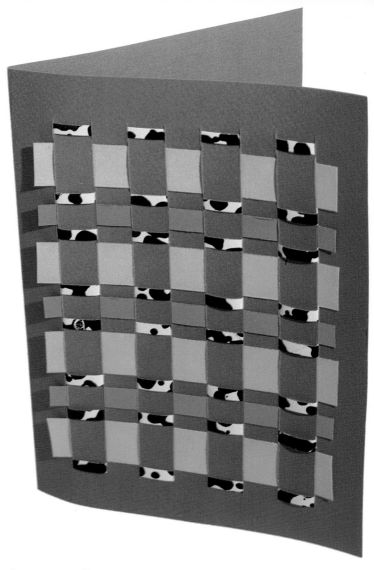

Letter Card and Gift Tag

Paste together two sheets of paper of different colors and fold in half. Using a craft knife, cut out the shape of a letter from the front of the card. Keep the letter that you cut out and punch a hole in it. Thread a piece of cord through the hole to make a gift tag.

Punch and Tear Card

Paste together two sheets of paper of different colors and fold in half to make a card. Pierce holes in the front of the card with a pencil and tear back strips of paper to make a pattern.

Cut Paper Card

Fold a sheet of colored paper in half. Using a craft knife, cut wavy slits and wavy shapes in the front of the card. Glue the shapes you cut out on the front of the card.

Gift Tags

Cut triangles or other shapes from colored paper. Punch holes in the tops of these shapes and thread a ribbon through. Write a message on the tag and attach it to a gift.

Here is a good way to use some of your decorated papers. When you have wrapped your gift, you can add ribbons, bows, and flowers to make it look special!

Wrapping a Parcel

Put the gift in the middle of the paper. Leave enough overlap at each end so that when you fold the ends over, the gift will be covered.

If possible, use double-sided tape that will not show.

Try to fold the ends as neatly as possible by making crisp corner folds.

The gift has been decorated with a paper curl. To make this, stick two strips of paper together and curl by wrapping them around the end of a wooden spoon or a broom handle.

Round Parcels

If you have a gift that is an awkward shape, such as a bottle, try putting it in a cardboard tube. Or wrap corrugated cardboard around it.

Wrap and glue decorated paper around the tube, leaving enough at the ends to fold under. Cut out two circles of paper and stick them over the ends to finish off.

Make paper curls and a pleated paper bow to decorate the parcel.

Paper Bow and Flower

Make a paper bow to decorate your parcel by cutting thin strips of paper and gluing the ends together. Stick four or more loops together and attach to your parcel. On page 22 you can find out how to make paper flowers.

First decide how big you want your shopping bag to be.

1. On the back of a sheet of decorated paper, draw out a plan like the one at the top of the page. The pieces marked "A" will be the sides of the bag and they should each be the same width. The pieces marked "B" will be the front and back of the bag. These should also equal each other, but be wider than "A". The pieces marked "C" will be the bottom of the bag. They should be slightly narrower than "A".

2. Cut out corners, as shown in picture 2. Use a scoring tool to score all the dotted lines marked. The height of the triangles – marked "X" – should equal half the width of the sides of the bag (also marked "X").

3. Fold over and glue the top of the bag. This makes a strong, neat edge.

4. You can either use a hole punch to punch holes for cord at the top of the bag (front and back), or you can make small slits to thread ribbon through.

1.

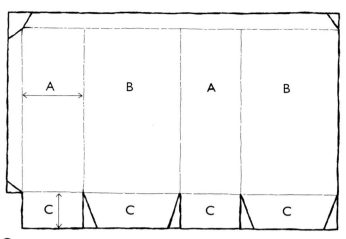

2.

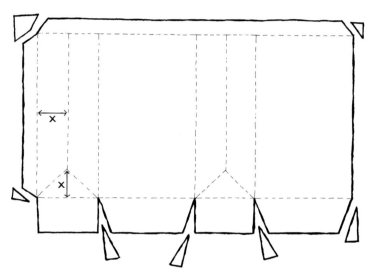

3.

4.

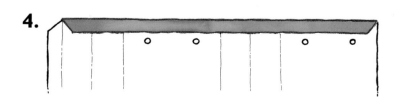

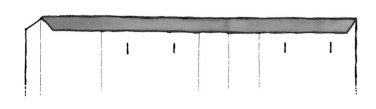

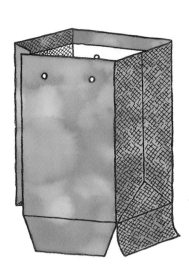

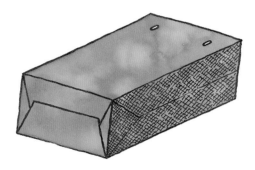

8. Slot cord or ribbon through the holes for handles.

5. Glue the bag together at the flap edge.

6. Fold the bottom flaps under and glue.

7. Gently push in the sides along the scored lines.

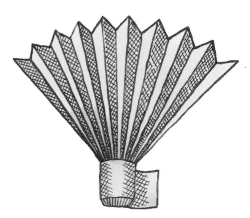

Here are some suggestions for making paper flowers, but try your own ideas too!

Pleat a strip of colored paper. Pinch one end together and glue a strip of paper around to hold it.

Cut a long strip of colored paper. Make cuts along the length, as shown above. Roll up the paper and bend the petals back. Try using different colored papers. Add leaves and a stem.

To make stems for your paper flowers, wrap a thin strip of green paper around a toothpick. Glue or tape the ends. You could also use a straw cut into short lengths and painted green.

Cut out different shapes for leaves, as shown above. Score down the center of each leaf and fold. Leaves are good for covering up joins between flowers and stems.

The flower shown above was made by cutting separate petals, overlapping them and gluing them together. The paper curls were made by wrapping thin strips of paper around a pencil.

Cut petal shapes in a long strip of paper, as shown above. Roll the flower up and fold back the petals. Tissue paper makes good roses. Try making different shapes of petals.

Woven Earrings

Cut some thin strips of paper of different colors. Weave the strips in and out. When you have made a woven square, cut out a piece of paper the same size and glue it to the back of the woven square. Glue an earring attachment to the back.

Pleated Brooch

Cut out two paper triangles. Pleat the triangles, as shown in the picture. Glue the long edges together. Pinch the pleats together in the middle. Wrap a thin strip of paper around the middle and glue it to hold the pleats in place. Glue a brooch attachment to the back.

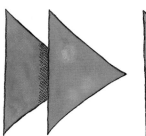

Triangle Earrings

Glue together two paper triangles of different colors. Curl the triangle around the handle of a wooden spoon. Make a second triangle like this. Pierce the top of each triangle and thread an earring attachment through them.

Accordion Bracelet

Take two long strips of paper. Glue the ends together at right angles. Keep folding one strip over the other, as shown in the picture. Glue the ends together. Accordion folds stretch and you should be able to slip the bracelet over your wrist easily.

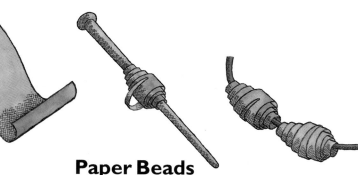

Paper Beads

Cut out a long, thin paper triangle. Starting at the wide end, roll the triangle around a knitting needle. Pull the needle out. Make a collection of beads and string them onto colored cord.

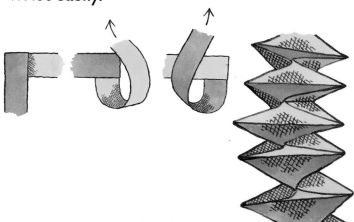

You should be able to find earring attachments in craft stores. You may also find barrettes, to which you can glue paper bows or flowers.

Papier-mâché means "paper pulp". You make it by building up layers of pasted paper.

First you will need to tear up many strips of paper – newspaper and colored paper. Use the paste recipe on page 10.

You can use your fingers to cover the strips of paper with paste, but an old paintbrush is less messy.

Making a Bowl

1. Cover a ball with plenty of Vaseline™. This will make the bowl easier to get off.

2. Paste on the first layer of torn paper using lots of paste on both sides of the paper. Do not go more than half way around the ball or the bowl will not come off!

3. Paste on 6 or 7 layers of paper to make the ball firm. Try to keep the layers even.

4. When the paper is dry, ask a grown-up to help cut around the edge of the bowl and gently lift it off.

You can use all sorts of things as basic molds to cover with papier-mâché. Large and small balls make good bowls, but you can also use paper or plastic cups, trays, or plates.

Whatever you use, cover it well with Vaseline™ first. This will make it easier to take the papier-mâché off when it is dry.

You can decorate papier-mâché by painting it when it is dry, or by using a pattern of colored paper for the final layer. If you are making a bowl, remember that the first layer you paste down will be the inside of the bowl!

These fish don't need feeding and you can make them any color you like! If you can't find a goldfish bowl, an old fish tank or a large glass jar will work just as well. Turn the page for the instructions.

Cut some simple fish shapes out of colored paper or thin cardboard. Using a craft knife, cut patterns in the fish or use a pencil to punch holes. Try gluing different colored cardboard behind the cutout shapes.

Next make a lid for your "aquarium." Turn your chosen container upside down onto a piece of cardboard and draw around it. Cut out the shape. Use Scotch™ tape to attach different lengths of thread to the fish and to the cardboard lid. Put the lid on the bowl and watch your fish swimming around!

You can make watery shapes by using the insides of envelopes, and strips of curled paper make good seaweed.

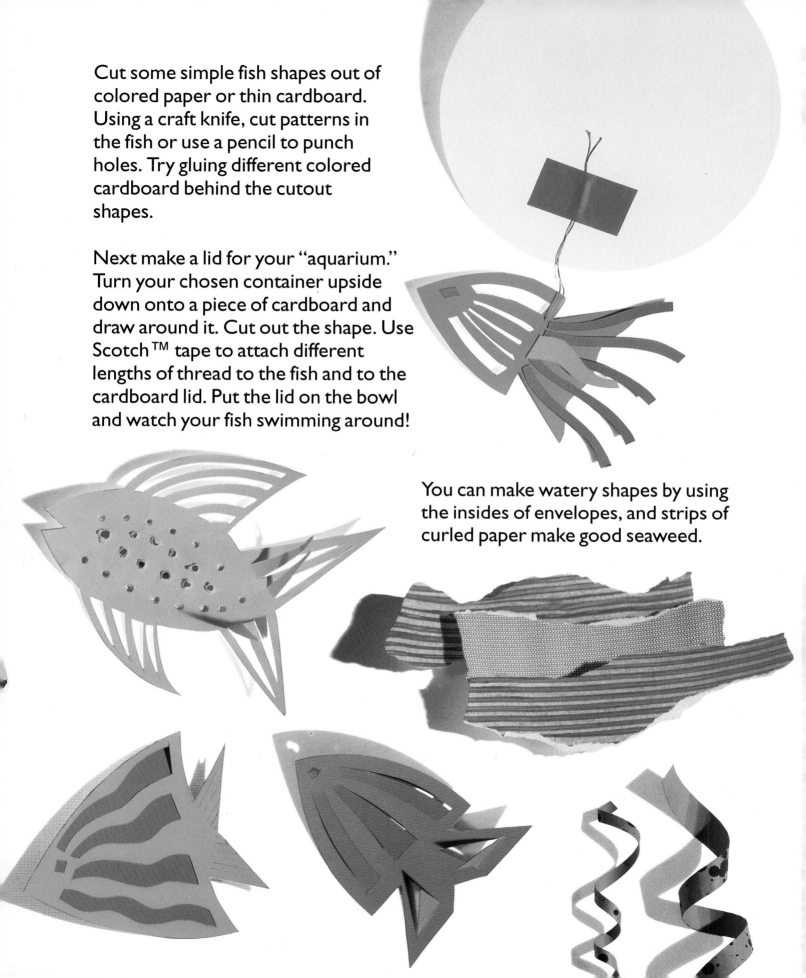